Bears

by Rich Linville

ISBN: 9798698858751

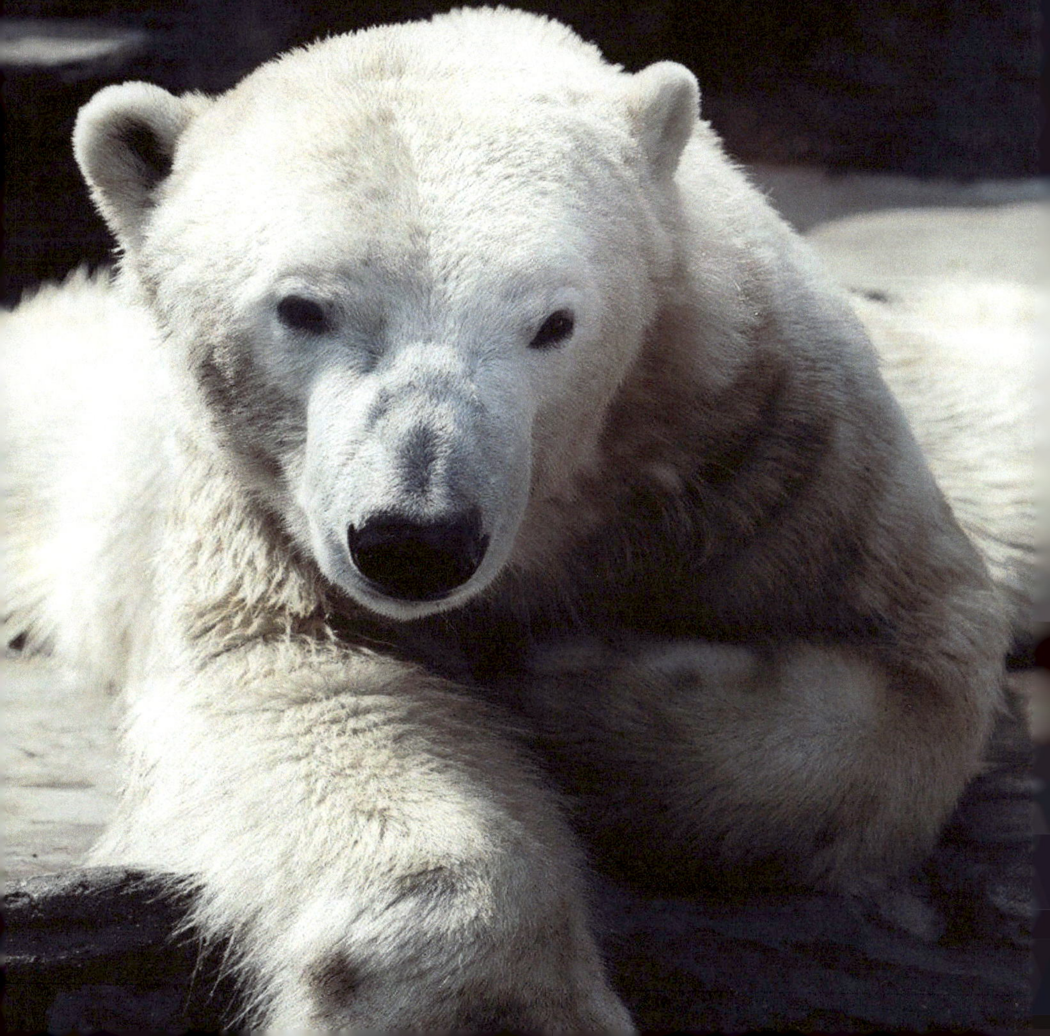

Modern bears are mammals with large bodies, short legs, small round ears, long noses, short tails, and shaggy hair.

On each paw, bears have 5 claws. They walk on four legs but can also stand and sit just like humans.

Of all the land animals, bears
have the best sense of smell.

They can smell 2,000 times farther than humans can smell. Bears can smell food up to 20 miles (32 kilometers) away.

Bears are usually solitary animals. They may be active in the daytime or the nighttime.

To save energy, some bears use logs or caves during the winter for a long, deep sleep (hibernation) up to 100 days. Never disturb a sleeping bear. They might attack you.

Bears are excellent runners and climbers.

Bears are exceptional
swimmers.

The 8 different kinds of bears today are: 1. Giant Panda, 2. Polar Bear, 3. Brown Bear, 4. Asian Black Bear,

1. Giant Panda

2. Polar Bear

3. Brown Bear

4. Asian Black Bear

5. American Black Bear,
6. Spectacled Bear,
7. Sloth Bear, and 8. Sun Bear.

5. American Black Bear

6. Spectacled Bear

7. Sloth Bear

8. Sun Bear

The giant panda is a bamboo plant eater (herbivore). The polar bear is a meat eater (carnivore). The brown bear, Asian black bear, American black bear, spectacled bear, sloth bear, and sun bear are both plant and meat eaters (omnivores).

The giant panda or panda bear is found in China. It has black patches around its eyes, ears, and across its body. Bamboo shoots and leaves make up most of its diet.

Small microbes in the panda's stomach are being studied for use in making biogas from bamboo and other plants to be used in vehicles like buses, cars and trucks.

The polar bear is found near the north pole. It is the largest kind of bear. Most polar bears are born on land and spend most of their time on ice looking for seals as food.

A female bear can have from
1 to 3 cubs every two years.
Cubs stay with their mother
for a little over a year. The
mother bear protects her cubs
and teaches them how to
hunt seals for food.

With the earth getting warmer, the ice sheets are melting. Polar bears are not able to hunt for food and are at risk.

The brown bear is found in Europe, Asia, and North America. They are also called grizzly bears. In some countries of Europe, the brown bear is a national or state animal.

If curious, alarmed or hungry, all bears can stand and walk a short distance.

In the wild and in zoos, there are crosses between grizzly bears and polar bears. They are known as pizzly bears or grolar bears.

The Asian black bear is also known as the moon bear, Asiatic black bear, and white-chested bear.

The Asian black bear is at risk because of humans clearing wide areas of trees (deforestation) and hunting for its body parts.

The American black bears usually live in forests. But, they will leave the forest in search of food. They are the most common bear in the world.

When first discovered by people, they only saw the black colored bear. Thus the name. However, black bears can also be brown, white, blue-gray, cinnamon, or blond.

The name spectacled (SPEK-tuh-kold) bear refers to the light colors on its head that look like spectacles or eyeglasses.

The spectacled bear is only found in South America.

Found mainly in India, the
sloth bear hunts for
termite and ant mounds.
Using their claws, they scrape
until they reach the combs of
these insects. The insects are
sucked up with a loud sound
that can be heard as far as the
length of two football fields.

The mother sloth bear will carry her cub on her back. After chewing different plants, the mother sloth bear vomits the mixture to feeds her cub. People of India call this "bear's bread" and think that it is delicious for them to eat.

Found in the tropical forests of Asia, the sun bear sunbathes and sleeps in trees high above the ground. They eat plants, insects, honey, and small animals.

The sun bear gets its name because it has a colorful chest pattern that looks like the sun.

Learn more about bears online or from books. Many bears are in danger of becoming extinct. Groups like the International Bear Association, and the Bear Specialist Group are concerned about saving bears.

What should you do if you see a bear?
1. Remain Calm.
Bears can sense fear.
2. Stand still and talk calmly so the bear knows you're there.
3. Hike in a group of at least three people.
4. Carry bear spray to spray in its eyes if it attacks you.
5. If a black bear attacks, fight back.
6. If a brown bear attacks, play dead by lying flat on your stomach with your hands behind your neck.

7. Never feed or take a selfie with any bear.

8. Bears can smell food from far away. Pack food in a bear canister or bear smell proof bags.

9. Change out of your clothes that have the smell of food.

10. Avoid cooking outside near bears.

11. Bears are dangerous but they tend to avoid humans.

Dedicated to my lovely wife Sulastri and my grandchildren Mia and Kai as well as everyone who enjoys learning about bears.

For over 40 years, I have enjoyed teaching at elementary, high school and college levels.

Please visit and follow my author page at: Amazon.com/author/richlinville

Illustrations from PixaBay, Wiki, and illustrations purchased from Edu-Clips.com.

Please check out my other books at bookstores and online under the name Rich Linville.

If you like unicorn jokes, you might enjoy:

Unicorn Jokes for Kids

24 Unicorn Jokes with Pictures

Written by Richard Linville
Illustrated by 1EverythingNice, et al.

My Alaskan Race
by Huskie Dog

Written by Rich Linville

My Basketball Blues

from the
Basketball's
Point of View
Written by Rich Linville

My Rocky Adventure!
By Rocky Magma
Written by Rich Linville

Someday I'd like to be
a rock instead of magma

www.ingramcontent.com/pod-product-compliance
Lightning Source LLC
Chambersburg PA
CBHW040930110726
48006CB00001B/129